American Girl®

Breakfast & Brunch

Photography **Nicole Hill Gerulat**

weldon**owen**

Contents

Best Meal of the Day!

You've heard it before: "Breakfast is the most important meal of the day." Although that statement may be true, when you wake up to delicious treats such as fluffy pancakes, blueberry waffles, maple-glazed bacon, coffee cake muffins, and whipped hot chocolate, you'll want to scream, "Breakfast is the *best* meal of the day!" This entire book is dedicated to the tastiest breakfast and brunch creations you could possibly think of.

In these pages, you'll find recipes for easy weekday breakfasts to cook up before you leave for school, as well as ones you can prepare the night before so that your mornings are a breeze. And when the weekend rolls around, it's all about brunch with friends and family. Ooey-gooey cinnamon rolls, cheesy breakfast pizzas, or an over-the-top biscuit bar are superfun for a casual gathering, while French crepes, mini scones, or bread pudding with pears are perfect for a fancy brunch. Tips scattered throughout the recipes tell you how to bring some of the dishes with you on the go, and helpful notes offer ideas for other tasty things to try.

From sleepover brunch buffets to bites that you can make ahead, the more than forty recipes in this book will make mornings so exciting that you'll never get bored of breakfast. A yummy homemade breakfast really is the best way to start your day!

How to use this book

Whether your family and friends have deemed you a cooking pro or making breakfast will be your first kitchen adventure, in this book you'll find plenty of recipes suited to your skill level. It begins with the basics, so you can master morning essentials such as scrambled eggs, muffins, pancakes, and waffles. From there, you'll learn how to make an array of sweet treats, some super-yummy options that are also good for you, and a selection of egg-cellent faves. Once you've got the basics down, you'll be able to move on to more involved dishes, which aren't necessarily more difficult—they just require a little more time and planning. Then round out your morning meals with a few tasty side dishes (hash browns, anyone?) and drinks. Before you know it, you'll be the best breakfast cook in town!

Cooking with care

When you see this symbol in the book, it means that you need an adult to help you with all or part of the recipe. Ask for help before continuing.

Adults have lots of culinary wisdom, and they can help keep you safe in the kitchen. Always have an adult assist you, especially if your recipe involves high heat, sharp objects, and electric appliances. Be sure to wash your hands before you begin cooking and after touching raw meat, poultry, eggs, or seafood.

Top breakfast tips

STAY ORGANIZED

Staying organized and paying attention are important cooking skills. Before you fire up the stovetop or oven, read the recipe, including the ingredient list, from start to finish. Then it's time to clear a clean surface and lay out all of your ingredients and tools. Once the food starts cooking, don't forget to set a timer!

GET HELP WITH SHARP TOOLS AND APPLIANCES

Make sure an adult helps you choose the correct knife for the task and that you're holding the handle firmly. When you're not using it, place it somewhere safe so it can't fall on the floor or be reached by younger siblings. Also have an adult assist you when using an electric mixer, blender, food processor, or other electric appliances, and keep them unplugged except when in use.

WATCH THE HEAT

Stovetop burners, hot ovens, boiling water—there's a lot of heat involved in cooking, so it's important to be very careful. Always use oven mitts when handling hot equipment and have an adult help you when you're cooking at the stovetop, moving things in and out of the oven, and working with hot liquids or foods.

Breakfast prep

With make-ahead options, such as Power-Packed Fig Bars (page 66) and Chia-Seed Pudding Jars (page 63), and superquick drinkable meals, like Fruit Smoothies (page 71), starting every day with a homemade breakfast that fills you up is totally doable! On the weekends, you can take time to make special morning treats to share with loved ones. Here are some thoughts to keep in mind.

★ PLAN AHEAD ★

Since breakfast is the first meal of the day, sometimes doing a little planning the day before goes a long way. Read the recipe you've chosen, make a grocery list, and go shopping with an adult to make sure that you have all the ingredients you need. Some dishes, such as Coffee Cake Muffins (page 28) and Tomato & Mozzarella Strata (page 110), can be prepared ahead of time and can be reheated in a low oven so you can serve them warm.

★ INVITE FRIENDS ★

Sleepovers are awesome, but breakfast-party sleepovers are even better! After a late night of party-riffic fun, you and your friends can work together to cook up some delicious food for the day. It beats sleeping in!

★ MAKE IT SPECIAL ★

Who doesn't love breakfast in bed? With an adult's assistance, you can put together a beautiful breakfast tray to surprise someone you love—for a birthday, Mother's Day, Father's Day, or just because. Add a little note and some flowers for an extra-special touch, and don't forget to carry the tray slowly and carefully so nothing spills.

The more the merrier

Making breakfast just got fun! Gather your friends to whip up delicious creations, like smoothies.

Breakfast Basics

Cinnamon Toast Cereal

Ever thought about making cereal from scratch? Believe it or not, you can! This is a fun kitchen project for a rainy day with friends. Make sure to roll out the dough as thinly as you can, and bake it long enough so the bits get crisp as they cool.

½ cup buttermilk

2 tablespoons maple syrup

1 teaspoon vanilla extract

1 cup all-purpose flour, plus more for dusting

1 cup whole-wheat flour

½ cup firmly packed light brown sugar

2 teaspoons ground cinnamon

1 teaspoon baking soda

¼ teaspoon salt

6 tablespoons (¾ stick) cold unsalted butter, cut into ½-inch cubes, plus 2 tablespoons, melted

3 tablespoons granulated sugar

 In a small bowl, whisk together the buttermilk, maple syrup, and vanilla.

Put the all-purpose flour, whole-wheat flour, brown sugar, 1 teaspoon of the cinnamon, the baking soda, and the salt in a food processor and pulse a few times to combine the ingredients. Scatter the butter cubes over the flour mixture and pulse until the butter is cut up into pieces the size of small peas. Drizzle the buttermilk mixture evenly over the flour mixture and pulse until a dough begins to form in clumps. (If mixing the ingredients by hand, use a pastry cutter or two dinner knives to cut in the butter until the mixture looks like rough bread crumbs. Add the remaining ingredients as instructed, then use your hands or a metal spoon to mix the dough until all ingredients are well combined.)

Lightly flour a clean work surface. Dump the dough onto the work surface and press it together with your hands. Divide the dough into 3 equal pieces and press each piece into a disk. Wrap each disk in plastic wrap and refrigerate for 30 minutes.

Preheat the oven to 350°F. Cut a sheet of parchment paper to fit on a cookie sheet. Lay the parchment on a work surface and lightly dust it with flour. Unwrap 1 dough disk and place it on the parchment, dust it with flour, and use a rolling pin to roll the dough into a rectangular shape about ⅛ inch thick or as thin as you can roll it, sprinkling with more flour as needed to prevent

~ *Continued on page 20* ~

~ Continued from page 18 ~

the dough from sticking. Using a pizza wheel or a sharp knife, trim the edges to straighten them; reserve the scraps. Cut the dough lengthwise into strips about ¾ inch wide, and then cut the strips crosswise into ¾-inch squares. (It's ok if your strips aren't perfectly straight.) Pierce each square a few times with a fork. Slide the parchment with the dough onto a cookie sheet.

In a small bowl, stir together the granulated sugar and the remaining 1 teaspoon cinnamon. Brush the dough gently and lightly with the melted butter, and then sprinkle evenly with the cinnamon sugar. Bake until lightly golden, about 13 minutes. Remove the cookie sheet from the oven, set it on a wire rack, and immediately re-cut the squares with a pizza wheel. Let cool completely on the cookie sheet on the wire rack. Meanwhile, roll out, cut, bake, and re-cut the remaining dough in the same way, adding the reserved scraps to the third piece of dough before rolling it out. When all of the cereal has cooled, break apart the squares. The cereal will keep in an airtight container at room temperature for up to 1 week.

Ricotta Pancakes with Spiced Bananas

Ricotta cheese—a soft, milky, slightly sweet cheese—and whipped egg whites give these pancakes a wonderfully light and fluffy texture. They're like eating clouds! The yummy banana topping is also delicious on waffles, crepes, or plain yogurt.

TOPPING

2 tablespoons all-purpose flour

1 tablespoon sugar

½ teaspoon ground cinnamon

¼ teaspoon freshly grated nutmeg

2 bananas, peeled and cut into ½-inch slices

1 tablespoon unsalted butter

PANCAKES

1 cup all-purpose flour

1 tablespoon baking powder

¼ teaspoon salt

1 cup ricotta cheese

⅔ cup whole milk

2 large eggs, separated

2 tablespoons sugar

Unsalted butter, for cooking

 To make the topping, in a medium bowl, combine the flour, sugar, cinnamon, and nutmeg. Add the banana slices, toss to coat on all sides, then transfer them to a plate, shaking off the excess coating. Line a large plate with paper towels and place it near the stove. Set a large frying pan over medium-high heat and add the butter. When the butter foams, add the banana slices in a single layer and fry until crisp, about 5 minutes, turning them halfway through. Transfer the bananas to the prepared plate to drain.

To make the pancakes, in a large bowl, whisk together the flour, baking powder, and salt. In a medium bowl, whisk together the ricotta, milk, and egg yolks. Add the ricotta mixture to the flour mixture and stir until blended. In a bowl, using an electric mixer, beat the egg whites and sugar on high speed until the egg whites hold stiff peaks when the beaters are lifted, about 2 minutes. Using a rubber spatula, fold the whites into the batter until combined.

Heat 2 teaspoons butter in a large nonstick frying pan over medium-high heat until melted and bubbly, tilting the pan to spread the butter evenly over the surface. For each pancake, pour 2 tablespoons batter onto the pan into a 3-inch round, spacing them about 1 inch apart. Cook until they bubble and the bottoms are golden brown, 1 to 2 minutes. Gently turn over and cook until golden brown on the second sides, 1 to 2 minutes longer. Transfer the pancakes to a serving plate, stacking them 3 or 4 high, spoon spiced bananas on top, and serve right away. Cook and serve the remaining pancakes in the same way.

Buttermilk Pancakes

Everyone knows that weekend mornings mean pancakes, and after sleeping in, there's nothing better than a tall, fluffy stack drizzled with warm maple syrup. Use pancake molds in fun shapes like hearts, stars, and flowers for a fancy touch.

2 large eggs

2 cups all-purpose flour, sifted

3 tablespoons sugar

2 teaspoons baking powder

1 teaspoon baking soda

1 teaspoon salt

2¼ cups buttermilk

4 tablespoons unsalted butter, melted, plus more for cooking the pancakes and serving

½ teaspoon vanilla extract

Maple syrup, for serving

 In a large bowl, whisk the eggs until frothy. Add the flour, sugar, baking powder, baking soda, salt, buttermilk, melted butter, and vanilla. Stir just until the batter is smooth and no lumps remain; do not overmix.

Set a large nonstick frying pan or griddle over medium heat and let the pan heat for about 2 minutes. Add 2 teaspoons butter to the pan and use a silicone spatula to spread it evenly over the surface. For each pancake, pour about ¼ cup batter into a round about 3 inches in diameter; space the pancakes about 1 inch apart. Cook until the edges of the pancakes begin to look dry and the bottoms are golden brown, about 2 minutes. Slide a thin spatula under each pancake, carefully flip it over, and cook until golden brown on the second side, about 1 minute longer. Using the spatula, transfer the pancakes to a serving plate, stacking them about 3 high, and serve right away with butter and maple syrup. Cook the remaining batter in the same way, serving each batch of pancakes when ready.

Note: If you're using pancake molds, follow the package directions for filling and cooking the batter.

Perfect Scrambled Eggs

Scrambled eggs is one of the quickest and easiest egg dishes you can make. These big, fluffy eggs paired with Maple-Glazed Bacon (page 120), buttery toast, and a glass of freshly squeezed orange juice are breakfast perfection.

8 large eggs

2 tablespoons whole milk

Pinch of salt

Pinch of ground black pepper

1½ tablespoons unsalted butter

Mix-ins (see box; optional)

 In a medium bowl, whisk the eggs, milk, salt, and pepper until nice and frothy, 1 to 2 minutes.

Place a medium nonstick frying pan over medium-low heat and add the butter. When the butter has melted, use a silicone spatula to spread it evenly over the surface. Pour in the eggs and cook without stirring until they just begin to set, about 1 minute. Using the spatula, gently stir the eggs around the pan, letting the uncooked egg run onto the surface of the pan. Continue to cook, stirring gently and constantly, until the eggs are set but still moist, 2 to 3 minutes longer. Transfer the eggs to a serving bowl or platter and serve right away.

Ideas for mix-ins

Veggies, *such as diced fresh tomatoes, sautéed diced zucchini, sautéed diced red onion, and chopped cooked spinach*

Shredded cheese, *such as Cheddar, Monterey jack, mozzarella, or Swiss*

Crumbled cooked sausage, *such as Italian sausage or chorizo*

Chopped fresh herbs, *such as flat-leaf parsley, chives, tarragon, or cilantro*

Note: *Stir in mix-ins at the end, just before the eggs are fully set.*

Keep it cool

Cook scrambled eggs over medium-low heat—a high heat can cause them to toughen or overcook.

Over easy
Flip eggs using a silicone spatula. It's a great tool for the task because it won't scratch your pan.

Easy Fried Eggs

From sunny-side up to over hard, fried eggs are a staple of the American breakfast table. And while making them might seem tricky, with the tips below you'll be able to flip an egg without breaking the yolk and cook it to perfection, just like a professional chef.

4 large eggs

Pinch of salt

Pinch of ground black pepper

2 tablespoons unsalted butter

 Crack the eggs into a bowl. Sprinkle the eggs with the salt and pepper.

Place a large nonstick pan over medium heat and add the butter. When the butter has melted, use a silicone spatula to spread it evenly over the surface. Gently pour in the eggs. For sunny-side-up eggs, cook the eggs without moving them until the whites are opaque, 2 to 3 minutes, and then remove the eggs with a spatula and serve right away. For over-easy, over-medium, or over-hard eggs, carefully slide a spatula under the eggs and gently flip them. (If you feel any resistance or the eggs begin to stick, run the spatula around the edge of the eggs until the eggs are free of the pan, then slide the spatula underneath.) Cook for about 30 seconds for over easy, 1 minute for over medium, and 1½ minutes for over-hard eggs; remove the eggs with the spatula and serve right away.

Tips for perfect fried eggs

Start with cold, fresh eggs right from the fridge—cold yolks stay intact and are more resilient, so they are less likely to break.

Crack the eggs into a bowl before sliding them into the pan to make sure you don't get any stray pieces of shell in your breakfast.

Let the pan warm up before you add the eggs so that they don't stick.

Coffee Cake Muffins

With a buttery crumb topping and pockets of sweet, sticky jam hiding inside, these muffins make mornings fun for everyone. Any type of jam is tasty here, so use your favorite. Coffee-Free Lattes (page 127) are a perfect drink to serve with these muffins.

TOPPING

¼ cup all-purpose flour

¼ cup firmly packed light brown sugar

3 tablespoons cold unsalted butter, cut into small chunks

MUFFINS

2 cups all-purpose flour

2 teaspoons baking powder

½ teaspoon baking soda

¼ teaspoon salt

½ cup (1 stick) unsalted butter, at room temperature

½ cup granulated sugar

2 large eggs

2 teaspoons vanilla extract

1 cup sour cream

¼ cup fruit jam (use your favorite type)

 Preheat the oven to 400°F. Line a standard 12-cup muffin pan with paper or foil liners.

To make the topping, in a small bowl, stir together the flour and brown sugar. Scatter the butter over the top and work it in with your fingertips until the mixture is evenly moistened and holds together when pinched. Put the topping in the freezer until needed.

To make the muffins, in a medium bowl, whisk together the flour, baking powder, baking soda, and salt. In a large bowl, using an electric mixer, beat the butter and granulated sugar on medium-high speed until fluffy, about 1 minute. Beat in the eggs, one at a time, and then add the vanilla and beat until well combined. Scrape down the bowl with a rubber spatula. Add the sour cream and beat on low speed to combine. Add the flour mixture and, using the rubber spatula, stir just until evenly moistened. The batter will be quite thick.

Fill each prepared muffin cup halfway full with batter. Drop 1 teaspoon jam onto the center of the batter in each cup. Divide the remaining batter evenly among the muffin cups, filling them almost to the rim. Sprinkle the muffins with the topping, dividing it evenly. Bake until golden brown and a wooden skewer inserted into the center of a muffin comes out clean, about 15 minutes. Remove from the oven and let cool in the pan on a wire rack for about 5 minutes, then carefully transfer them directly to the rack. Serve warm.

Pumpkin Spice Muffins

These muffins are perfect for a fall or winter breakfast or brunch, but we love to make them all year round. Be sure to use pure pumpkin purée, not pumpkin pie mix, which contains sugar and spices. Add a walnut topping (below) to make them extra fancy.

1½ cups all-purpose flour

1 teaspoon baking soda

½ teaspoon baking powder

½ teaspoon salt

½ teaspoon ground cinnamon

½ teaspoon ground cloves

½ teaspoon ground nutmeg

1½ cups sugar

1 cup canned pumpkin purée

½ cup canola oil

2 large eggs

1 tablespoon finely grated orange zest

½ teaspoon vanilla extract

 Preheat the oven to 350°F. Line a standard 12-cup muffin pan with paper or foil liners.

In a medium bowl, whisk together the flour, baking soda, baking powder, salt, cinnamon, cloves, and nutmeg. In a large bowl, whisk together the sugar, pumpkin, oil, eggs, orange zest, and vanilla until well combined. Add the flour mixture and whisk gently just until blended.

Divide the batter evenly among the prepared muffin cups. Bake until a wooden skewer inserted into the center of a muffin comes out clean, about 20 minutes. Remove from the oven and let cool in the pan on a wire rack for about 5 minutes, then carefully transfer them directly to the rack. Let cool completely and serve.

Walnut topping

In a small bowl, stir together 3 tablespoons firmly packed light brown sugar, 2 tablespoons all-purpose flour, and ¼ teaspoon each ground nutmeg and ground cinnamon. Add ¼ cup chopped walnuts and mix well. Add 1 tablespoon unsalted butter (at room temperature) and, using your fingertips, rub it into the mixture until blended. Right before baking, sprinkle the topping over the batter, dividing it evenly.

Basic Waffles

Waffles are a fun dish to serve at a breakfast or brunch party because guests can add their favorite toppings. Set out bowls of fresh berries, sliced bananas, and whipped cream, along with maple syrup in a big pitcher, for the ultimate waffle spread.

2 cups all-purpose flour

1 tablespoon sugar

1 tablespoon baking powder

¼ teaspoon salt

3 large eggs

1½ cups whole milk

6 tablespoons (¾ stick) unsalted butter, melted

Maple syrup, for serving

 Preheat a waffle maker.

In a medium bowl, whisk together the flour, sugar, baking powder, and salt. In a large bowl, using an electric mixer, whisk the eggs until light and frothy, then whisk in the milk and melted butter. While whisking gently, gradually add the flour mixture and mix just until combined. The batter will be lumpy.

When the waffle maker is ready, pour batter over the cooking grid. Close the lid and cook until the steam subsides or the indicator light signals that the waffle is ready, 2 to 4 minutes. Carefully open the lid, transfer the waffle to a serving plate, and serve right away with maple syrup. Cook the remaining batter in the same way, serving each waffle as it's ready.

Variation: Lemon-Poppy Seed Waffles

In a medium bowl, whisk together 2 large eggs, 1½ cups buttermilk, ½ cup melted unsalted butter, 1 teaspoon vanilla extract, and 2 tablespoons each of finely grated lemon zest and fresh lemon juice. In a large bowl, whisk together 1½ cups all-purpose flour, ⅓ cup sugar, 2 tablespoons poppy seeds, 1½ teaspoons baking powder, 1 teaspoon baking soda, and ¼ teaspoon salt. Make a well in the center of the dry ingredients, pour in the buttermilk mixture, and whisk gently just until combined. Then cook the batter as directed above.

Whole Wheat–Blueberry Waffles

These delicious, good-for-you waffles are tie-dyed with swirls of dark blue. The berries tend to burn easily, so use the medium-low heat setting on the waffle maker, and carefully wipe the grid with paper towels between batches to remove any residue.

2 large eggs

1½ cups whole milk

½ cup canola oil

¾ cup all-purpose flour

¾ cup whole-wheat flour

2 tablespoons firmly packed light brown sugar

1 tablespoon baking powder

½ teaspoon ground cinnamon

¼ teaspoon salt

1 cup fresh or thawed frozen blueberries

Maple syrup, for serving

 Preheat a waffle maker on the medium-low setting.

In a medium bowl, whisk together the eggs, milk, and oil. In a large bowl, whisk together the all-purpose flour, whole-wheat flour, brown sugar, baking powder, cinnamon, and salt. Make a well in the center of the dry ingredients, pour in the milk mixture, and whisk gently just until combined but with a few lumps. Using a rubber spatula, gently fold in the blueberries.

When the waffle maker is ready, spoon batter over the cooking grid; spread the batter so that it almost reaches the edges of the grid. Close the lid and cook until the steam subsides or the indicator light signals that the waffle is ready, 3 to 4 minutes. Carefully open the lid and transfer the waffle to a serving plate; serve right away with maple syrup. Carefully wipe the waffle maker grid with paper towels and cook the remaining batter in the same way, serving each waffle as it's ready.

Surprise!
There's no better
surprise than
breakfast-in-bed.
A handwritten card
is an extra-sweet
touch.

Strawberry Jam Muffins

Who doesn't love spreading jam on fresh-out-of-the-oven baked goods? Now you can have your jam and eat it too—but the jam is tucked inside these breakfast treats! The sour cream in the batter makes these muffins extra moist and delicious.

2 cups all-purpose flour

¾ cup sugar

1 tablespoon
baking powder

½ teaspoon
baking soda

½ teaspoon salt

2 large eggs

1¼ cups sour cream

6 tablespoons (¾ stick)
unsalted butter,
melted

1 teaspoon vanilla
extract

½ cup strawberry jam

 Preheat the oven to 375°F. Line a standard 12-cup muffin pan with paper or foil liners.

In a large bowl, whisk together the flour, sugar, baking powder, baking soda, and salt. In a medium bowl, whisk together the eggs, sour cream, melted butter, and vanilla until smooth. Add the egg mixture to the flour mixture and stir just until evenly moistened. The batter will be slightly lumpy.

Spoon batter into the prepared muffin cups, filling each about one-third full. Drop 2 teaspoons jam onto the center of the batter in each cup. Divide the remaining batter evenly among the muffin cups, filling them almost to the rim. Bake until golden brown and a wooden skewer inserted into the center of a muffin comes out clean, 20 to 25 minutes. Remove from the oven and let the muffins cool in the pan on a wire rack for about 5 minutes, then carefully transfer them directly to the rack. Let cool for few minutes longer and serve warm or at room temperature.

Super creamy

If you don't have sour cream in the fridge, you can substitute whole-milk Greek yogurt instead.

Packable snack

Muffins travel well and don't require a fork to eat, so they're a perfect choice for taking breakfast to go.

Mini Blueberry-Oat Muffins

Toasting the oats brings out their flavor and adds a subtle nutty taste. You can use fresh or frozen blueberries (thaw them first), so this is a great recipe to make at any time of year. Don't break the berries when you stir them or you'll end up with blue-gray muffins.

1¼ cups quick-cooking rolled oats

1 cup all-purpose flour

¾ cup sugar

½ teaspoon ground cinnamon

1 teaspoon baking powder

½ teaspoon baking soda

½ teaspoon salt

1 large egg

1 cup buttermilk

4 tablespoons (½ stick) unsalted butter, melted

1 cup fresh or thawed frozen blueberries

 Preheat the oven to 400°F. Line a 24-cup mini muffin pan with paper or foil liners.

Put the oats in a medium frying pan and set the pan over medium heat. Toast the oats, stirring constantly with a wooden spoon, until fragrant and just beginning to brown, 4 to 5 minutes. Remove from the heat and let cool slightly.

Pour the cooled oats into a large bowl. Add the flour, sugar, cinnamon, baking powder, baking soda, and salt and whisk to combine. In a medium bowl, whisk together the egg, buttermilk, and melted butter. Pour the buttermilk mixture into the dry ingredients and mix with a wooden spoon just until evenly moistened. Gently stir in the blueberries.

Divide the batter evenly among the prepared muffin cups, filling them nearly to the rim. Bake until lightly browned and a wooden skewer inserted into the center of a muffin comes out clean, 12 to 14 minutes. Let the muffins cool in the pan on a wire rack for about 5 minutes, then carefully transfer them directly to the rack. Let cool for a few minutes longer and serve warm or at room temperature.

Sweet Treats

Cinnamon Rolls with Cream Cheese Icing

Cinnamon rolls baking in the oven is one of the best smells ever! These are downright irresistible. You can make the dough and shape the rolls the night before so that all you have to do in the morning is take them out of the refrigerator and bake them.

DOUGH

1 cup whole milk

½ cup granulated sugar

5 tablespoons unsalted butter, melted, plus more for greasing the bowl and baking pan

3 large eggs

1 package (2½ teaspoons) quick-rise yeast

4½ cups all-purpose flour, plus more as needed

1¼ teaspoons salt

FILLING

½ cup firmly packed light brown sugar

2 teaspoons ground cinnamon

6 tablespoons (¾ stick) unsalted butter, at room temperature

To make the dough, in the bowl of a stand mixer, combine the milk, sugar, melted butter, eggs, and yeast and whisk until blended. Add 4½ cups of the flour and the salt. Attach the flat beater to the stand mixer and mix on medium-low speed, adding up to ½ cup flour to make a soft dough that does not stick to the bowl. Remove the flat beater and fit the stand mixer with the dough hook attachment. Knead the dough on medium-low speed, adding more flour if needed, until the dough is smooth but still soft, 6 to 7 minutes. Remove the dough from the bowl and shape it into a ball. Brush a large bowl with melted butter. Add the dough to the bowl and turn to coat its entire surface with butter. Cover with plastic wrap and let rise in a warm place until the dough has doubled in bulk, 1½ to 2 hours.

While the dough is rising, make the filling: In the stand-mixer bowl, combine the brown sugar, cinnamon, and butter. Attach the flat beater and beat on medium speed until combined, about 30 seconds. Set aside.

When the dough has doubled in bulk, use your hand to gently punch down and deflate the dough. Lightly flour a clean work surface. Turn the dough out onto the floured surface and dust the top with flour. Using a rolling pin, roll out the dough to a 16-by-14-inch rectangle, with a long side facing you. Spread the filling evenly over the dough, leaving a 1-inch uncovered border at the top and bottom. Starting at the long side of the rectangle farthest from you, roll up the rectangle into a log. Pinch the seam to seal. Using a sharp

~ Continued on page 44 ~

Try this!

Sprinkle ½ cup raisins, dried cherries, or chopped pecans over the filling before rolling up the dough.

~ Continued from page 43 ~

knife, cut the log crosswise into 8 equal slices. Brush a 9-by-13-inch baking pan with melted butter. Arrange the slices, cut side up, in the pan, spacing them evenly. Cover loosely with plastic wrap and let rise in a warm place until doubled in bulk, 1¼ to 1½ hours. (If making the night before, refrigerate for 8 to 12 hours; remove from the refrigerator 1 hour before baking.)

Preheat the oven to 350°F.

Bake until the rolls are golden brown, about 30 minutes. Remove from the oven and let cool in the pan on a wire rack for 15 minutes.

Meanwhile, make the icing: Sift the powdered sugar into a medium bowl and add the cream cheese, butter, vanilla, and orange zest. Using an electric mixer, beat the mixture on low speed until crumbly. Gradually beat in the milk. The icing should be very thick but pourable; if needed, beat in more milk, 1 teaspoon at a time, until the icing has the correct consistency. Drizzle the icing over the warm rolls, or pour it over the rolls and use a butter knife to spread it out evenly. Let cool for at least 15 minutes. Serve the rolls warm or at room temperature.

ICING

1½ cups powdered sugar

2 ounces cream cheese, at room temperature

2 tablespoons unsalted butter, at room temperature

½ teaspoon vanilla extract

Finely grated zest of 1 orange

¼ cup whole milk, plus more as needed

Lemon Quick Bread

Fresh lemons are easy to find year-round, so you can bake this flavorful, easy-to-make quick bread any time you want. Cutting a few slits into the warm loaf before pouring on the glaze allows the glaze to seep deep inside the bread, filling it with yumminess.

BREAD

1½ cups all-purpose flour

¾ cup sugar

1 teaspoon baking powder

¼ teaspoon baking soda

Finely grated zest of 1 large lemon

Pinch of salt

2 large eggs

½ cup whole milk

¼ cup canola oil

1 teaspoon vanilla extract

GLAZE

⅓ cup sugar

Juice of 1 large lemon

 Preheat the oven to 350°F. Lightly coat a 9-by-5-inch loaf pan with nonstick cooking spray.

To make the bread, in a large bowl, whisk together the flour, sugar, baking powder, baking soda, lemon zest, and salt. In a medium bowl, whisk together the eggs, milk, oil, and vanilla until well blended. Pour the egg mixture into the flour mixture. Using a rubber spatula, mix just until combined; the batter will be thick and slightly lumpy. Pour the batter into the prepared pan and smooth the top with the rubber spatula; the pan will be about half full.

Bake until the bread is deep golden brown with some cracks on the surface and a butter knife inserted into the center comes out clean, about 40 minutes. Remove from the oven and set on a wire rack. Insert the butter knife vertically into the bread in 8 to 10 uniformly spaced places. Let cool while you make the glaze.

To make the glaze, combine the sugar and lemon juice in a small saucepan and bring to a boil over medium-high heat. Continue to boil, stirring once or twice, until the mixture is bubbling and frothy on the surface, about 3 minutes. Remove from the heat and immediately pour the glaze evenly over the warm bread. Let the loaf cool completely in the pan on the rack.

Run a thin knife around the inside edge of the pan to loosen the loaf. Carefully turn it out directly onto the rack. Turn upright, cut into slices, and serve.

Bite-Sized Berry Scones

There are three secrets to ensuring these British-style treats are (1) make sure the butter and buttermilk are cold, (2) use a gentle touch when kneading the dough, and (3) work quickly to prevent the dough from becoming too soft.

SCONES

3 cups all-purpose flour, plus more for dusting

3 tablespoons granulated sugar

2½ teaspoons baking powder

½ teaspoon baking soda

½ teaspoon salt

10 tablespoons (1¼ sticks) cold unsalted butter, cut into ½-inch pieces

¾ cup dried cranberries, dried blueberries, or dried currants

1 cup cold buttermilk

GLAZE

¾ cup powdered sugar, sifted

1 tablespoon whole milk or water, plus more as needed

 Preheat the oven to 425°F. Line a cookie sheet with parchment paper.

In a large bowl, whisk together the flour, granulated sugar, baking powder, baking soda, and salt. Scatter the butter pieces over the flour mixture and toss to coat. Using a pastry blender or 2 dinner knives, cut the butter into the dry ingredients until the mixture forms crumbs about the size of small peas. Stir in the dried berries. Pour in the buttermilk and stir with a fork or rubber spatula just until combined.

Sprinkle a clean work surface with flour and turn the dough out onto the floured surface. With floured hands, gently knead the dough 8 to 10 times; the dough will be very soft. Press and pat the dough into a rectangle about ¾ inch thick. Using a 1½-inch biscuit cutter or shaped cookie cutter, cut out as many rounds of dough as possible. Gather up the scraps, knead briefly, and pat to ¾ inch thick. Cut out more rounds and place them on the prepared cookie sheet, spacing them evenly.

Bake until the edges are golden brown, about 10 minutes. Remove from the oven and carefully transfer them to a wire rack to cool.

To make the glaze, in a small bowl, whisk the powdered sugar and milk until smooth; it should be thick but pourable. If needed, whisk in additional milk 1 teaspoon at a time. Brush or drizzle over the warm scones. Let stand for at least 10 minutes to allow the glaze to set. Serve warm or at room temperature.

On the side
Mixed berries make a delicious and colorful accompaniment to these roll-ups—or serve them with a luscious fruit salad (page 75).

French Toast Roll-Ups

This is a superfun spin on classic French toast. These roll-ups look like they are hard to make, but they are surprisingly simple. Just spread the filling on the bread, roll the slices up tightly, dip them in beaten egg, and cook _____ brown.

8 large slices good-quality whole-wheat or white sandwich bread

8 tablespoons whipped cream cheese

8 teaspoons fruit jam (use your favorite type)

2 large eggs

2 tablespoons whole milk

1 tablespoon unsalted butter

Maple syrup, cinnamon sugar, or powdered sugar, for serving (optional)

 Trim the crust off of each slice of bread. Using _____ down on the bread slices to flatten them slightly. Lay a bread slice with a short end facing you. Spread 1 tablespoon of the cream cheese on the bread in a thin, even layer all the way to the edges. Spread 1 teaspoon jam on top of the cream cheese in a thin, even layer, leaving the top 1 inch free of jam. Starting at the end closest to you, tightly roll up the bread. Repeat with the remaining bread slices, cream cheese, and jam.

In a shallow bowl, whisk the eggs and milk until frothy. Dip each roll-up in the egg mixture, coating it on all sides, and set aside on a plate.

Place a large nonstick frying pan over medium-low heat and add the butter. When the butter has melted, add the roll-ups in a single layer and cook, turning often, until golden brown on all sides, about 5 minutes total. Transfer the roll-ups to individual plates. If you like, drizzle with maple syrup, sprinkle with cinnamon sugar, or spoon some powdered sugar in a fine-mesh sieve and dust the roll-ups. Serve right away.

More ways to roll!

Swap the cream cheese and jam for Nutella and 1 tablespoon chopped fresh raspberries, or peanut butter and 1 tablespoon chopped bananas. Then roll, dip, and cook the roll-ups according to the directions above.

Cinnamon-Sugar Donut Holes

Surprise! You don't have to go to the trouble of making classic ring-shaped donuts to get donut holes! Invite friends over so you have lots of hands to help shape the dough. You can use the same recipe to make powdered-sugar and confetti versions (page 52).

2¼ cups all-purpose flour

2 teaspoons ground cinnamon

1½ teaspoons baking powder

½ teaspoon salt

2 large eggs

1½ cups granulated sugar

½ cup whole milk

2 tablespoons unsalted butter, melted

1 teaspoon vanilla extract

Canola or peanut oil, for brushing and deep-frying

 In a bowl, whisk together the flour, 1 teaspoon of the cinnamon, the baking powder, and the salt. In a large bowl, using an electric mixer, beat the eggs and ½ cup of the granulated sugar on low speed until creamy and pale, about 3 minutes. Turn off the mixer. Add half of the flour mixture and beat on low speed just until incorporated. Turn off the mixer and scrape down the bowl with a rubber spatula. Add the milk, melted butter, and vanilla and beat on low speed until well blended. Turn off the mixer. Add the remaining flour mixture and beat, still on low speed, just until the mixture comes together into a soft dough. Cover the bowl with plastic wrap and refrigerate until the dough is firm, at least 30 minutes or up to 1 hour.

Line a cookie sheet with waxed paper and brush the paper with oil. Line a second cookie sheet with paper towels. Pour oil to a depth of 2 inches into a deep-fryer or a large, heavy-bottomed saucepan and warm over medium-high heat until the oil registers 360°F on a deep-frying thermometer.

Meanwhile, lightly oil the palms of your hands. Pull off about 1 tablespoon of the dough and roll it between your palms into a smooth ball about 1 inch in diameter. Place it on the oiled paper. Shape the remaining dough in the same way, spacing the dough balls about 1 inch apart on the cookie sheet. You should have about 40 dough balls.

~ *Continued on page 52* ~

~ Continued from page 50 ~

Try this!

Donut holes are also tasty the next day. Just warm them on a cookie sheet for 5 to 7 minutes in a 300°F oven.

Using tongs and handling only 1 at a time, carefully transfer 6 to 8 donut holes from the cookie sheet to the hot oil, gently placing them in. Don't overcrowd the pan. The donut holes should float to the top and puff to about double their size. Deep-fry until deep golden brown on the first side, about 1½ minutes. Using a slotted spoon, tongs, or a wire skimmer, turn each donut hole and fry until deep golden brown on the second side, about 1 minute longer. Transfer to the paper towel–lined cookie sheet to drain. Fry the remaining donut holes in the same way, allowing the oil to return to 360°F between batches.

In a wide, shallow bowl, stir together the remaining 1 teaspoon cinnamon and 1 cup granulated sugar. When the donut holes are cool enough to handle but still slightly warm, roll them in the cinnamon sugar until evenly coated and serve.

Powdered-Sugar Donut Holes Follow the recipe for Cinnamon-Sugar Donut Holes, replacing the cinnamon sugar with 1 cup sifted powdered sugar and coating the warm donut holes as directed.

Confetti Donut Holes In a medium bowl, whisk 2 cups powdered sugar, ½ teaspoon salt, ½ cup whole milk, and 2 teaspoons vanilla extract until smooth and well blended. Follow the recipe for Cinnamon-Sugar Donut Holes to make and fry the donut holes. When cool enough to handle, dip a few at a time into the glaze to coat evenly on all sides. Decorate with sprinkles and serve.

Vanilla-Glazed "Toaster" Pastries

These pastries might look like the kind you can buy in a box, but the fresh-fruit filling makes them even more delish—and better for you, too. You can eat them at room temperature, or reheat them on a cookie sheet for a few minutes in a 300°F oven.

PASTRIES

1 large egg

2 cups fresh pitted cherries or blueberries

3 tablespoons sugar

½ teaspoon grated lemon zest

2 teaspoons lemon juice

⅛ teaspoon ground cinnamon (optional)

1 sheet frozen puff pastry, thawed

All-purpose flour, for dusting

GLAZE

¾ cup plus 2 tablespoons powdered sugar

2½ tablespoons water

½ teaspoon vanilla extract

 Preheat the oven to 350°F. Line a cookie sheet with parchment paper. In a small bowl, beat the egg with a fork.

In a medium bowl, combine the fruit, sugar, lemon zest, lemon juice, and ground cinnamon (if using). Set aside.

Place the puff pastry on a clean, lightly floured work surface. Using a rolling pin, roll out the pastry until it is a square that is ⅛ inch thick. Cut the pastry into 4 equal squares, then cut each square in half to make a total of 8 rectangles.

Place 2 dough rectangles on the prepared cookie sheet. Brush the edges of 1 rectangle with beaten egg, then spoon one-fourth of the fruit mixture onto the dough, leaving a ½-inch border uncovered. Using a knife, cut vents into the top of a second rectangle and carefully place it over the first one, sealing the fruit inside. Using the tines of a fork, crimp the edges. Repeat to form 3 more pastries on the cookie sheet.

Bake until the pastries are golden brown, about 25 minutes. Remove from the oven and let cool completely on the cookie sheet on a wire rack.

To make the glaze, in a small bowl, whisk the powdered sugar, water, and vanilla until smooth. Drizzle the glaze evenly over the pastries and serve.

French Crepes with Jam

Crepes might sound fancy, but they're actually easy to make. Use your favorite types of fruit jam as fillings and serve the crepes as they are made. Or try the out-of-this-world Banana-Filled Crepes with Chocolate Sauce (page 56).

2 large eggs

2 cups whole milk

2 tablespoons unsalted butter, melted, plus more for cooking the crepes

1½ cups all-purpose flour

1 tablespoon granulated sugar

½ teaspoon baking powder

½ teaspoon vanilla extract

½ teaspoon salt

Assorted fruit jams

Powdered sugar, for dusting

Crack the eggs into a bowl. Pour the milk into a blender. Add the eggs, pour in the melted butter, and add the flour, granulated sugar, baking powder, vanilla, and salt. Blend for a few seconds to mix. Turn off the blender. Using a rubber spatula, scrape down the sides of the blender, then blend again until smooth, a few seconds longer. Rest the batter for about 5 minutes before using.

Set a 10-inch crepe pan or nonstick frying pan over medium-high heat and let the pan get hot. Add 1 teaspoon butter to the pan and, using a silicone spatula, spread it evenly over the surface. Pour about ⅓ cup crepe batter all at once into the pan and immediately tilt and swirl the pan so that the batter evenly covers the entire surface of the pan. Cook the crepe until lightly browned on the bottom (you can lift an edge with the spatula to take a peek), about 2 minutes. Carefully slide the spatula under the center of the crepe and flip the crepe. While the second side is cooking, scoop a spoonful of jam onto the center of the crepe. When the second side is lightly browned, after about 2 minutes, slip the crepe, jam side up, onto a serving plate. Spread the jam evenly over the crepe, then fold the crepe into quarters, forming a triangle shape. Sprinkle the crepe with powdered sugar and serve right away. Cook the remaining batter, fill, and serve the crepes in the same way, serving each crepe when it's ready.

Banana-Filled Crepes with ~~Chocolate Sauce~~

The streets of Paris are lined with vendors selling fresh, hot crepes with many different fillings. One of the most popular is Nutella and sliced bananas. Once you've mastered making the crepes on page 55, try our twist on this French favorite.

SAUCE

¾ cup heavy cream

4 ounces bittersweet chocolate, coarsely chopped

FILLING

2 tablespoons unsalted butter

2 ripe but firm bananas, peeled and cut into ½-inch-thick slices

1 tablespoon firmly packed light brown sugar

¼ cup toasted, skinned, and chopped hazelnuts (optional)

 To make the sauce, pour the cream into a small saucepan and bring to a simmer over medium heat. Remove from the heat and add the chocolate. Let stand for 3 minutes, then whisk until smooth. Cover to keep warm and set aside.

To make the filling, put the butter in a medium frying pan and set the pan over medium heat. When the butter has melted, add the bananas and cook, stirring gently, until heated through, about 2 minutes. Add the brown sugar and cook until it dissolves, about 1 minute. Remove from the heat.

Make the crepes as directed on page 55, eliminating the jam steps. Place 1 fully cooked crepe on a clean work surface. Place a few caramelized banana slices on the lower right quadrant of the crepe. Fold the crepe in half from left to right to cover the bananas, and then fold in half again from top to bottom to form a triangle shape. Repeat with the remaining crepes and bananas.

To serve, drizzle with chocolate sauce, sprinkle with toasted hazelnuts, if you like, and serve right away.

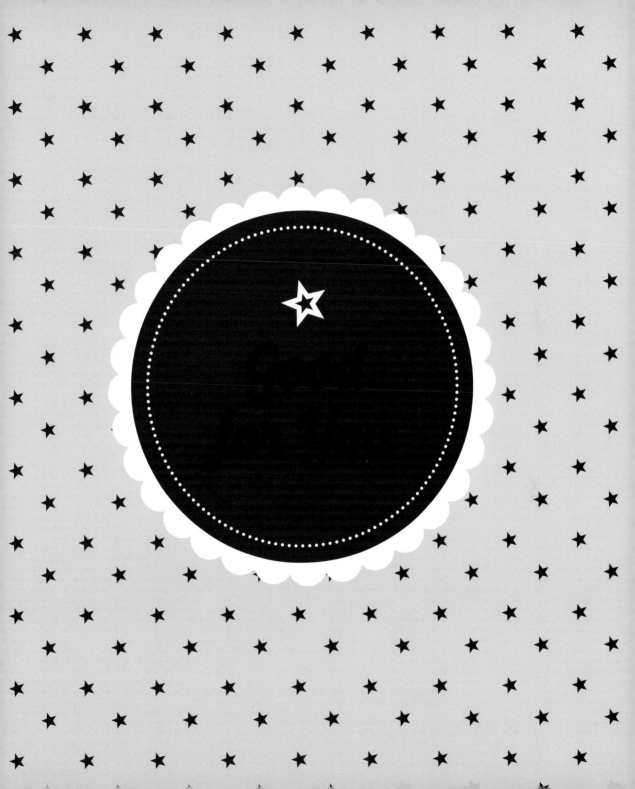

Açaí Bowls

Açaí (pronounced "ah-sigh-EE") is a nutrient-rich, tart-sweet berry from Brazil. The purple-red fruit is sold as a frozen purée in packets, so it's perfect for making smoothies and a thick, creamy, spoonable mixture that's topped with fruits and coconut.

AÇAÍ PURÉE

1 packet frozen açaí

1 large banana, peeled, roughly chopped, and frozen

1 cup frozen strawberries, blueberries, blackberries, raspberries, or a combination

¼ cup mango juice or other juice of your choice

Toppings (see box)

 To make the açaí purée, add the frozen açaí, chopped banana, frozen berries, and juice to a blender and blend until very smooth. Scrape the mixture into 2 bowls, dividing it evenly.

Top the açaí purée with your choice of toppings, such as fresh berries, mango slices, banana pieces, kiwi slices, coconut, and chopped nuts or seeds, if you like, evenly dividing the ingredients. Serve right away.

Ideas for toppings

Fresh blueberries, blackberries, raspberries, or strawberries, *add ¼ cup, whole or halved*

Mango, *add ½ cup, peeled and thinly sliced*

Banana, *add ½ cup, peeled and thinly sliced*

Kiwi, *peeled and thinly sliced*

Coconut, *2 to 3 tablespoons shredded or flaked, lightly toasted*

Chopped pecans or sliced almonds, *2 to 3 tablespoons, toasted (optional)*

Hemp seeds, flaxseeds, or chia seeds, *2 teaspoons*

Chia-Seed Pudding Jars with Fresh Fruit

Chia seeds are easy to prepare and packed with good-for-you nutrients. To make this deliciously creamy dish perfect for a brunch party, attach a pretty name tag to the jar for each guest. If you like, swap almond milk for the coconut milk, or use a combo of both.

1 cup canned coconut milk

¼ cup chia seeds

2 tablespoons maple syrup

Vanilla extract

4 cups blueberries, sliced strawberries, diced mango, or a combination

¼ cup toasted coconut chips

 In each of 4 pint-sized jars, stir together ¼ cup coconut milk, 1 tablespoon chia seeds, 1½ teaspoons maple syrup, and a dash of vanilla. Cover and refrigerate until set, at least 4 hours or up to overnight.

Spoon 1 cup of fruit on top of the pudding in each jar. Sprinkle each with 1 tablespoon coconut chips and serve right away.

Breakfast on the go! Assembled in pint-sized glass jars and sealed with secure-fitting lids, these individual puddings are perfect when you need a healthy (and yummy) breakfast or snack that travels well. Don't forget to pack a spoon!

Quinoa & Berry Breakfast Bowls

Quinoa (pronounced "KEEN-wah") is a superhealthy grainlike seed that can be made into a tasty breakfast, kind of like oatmeal. You can use any type for this recipe—white, red, or even rainbow. Rinse it well before cooking to remove some of its bitterness.

1 cup quinoa

3 cups vanilla almond milk, plus more as needed

¼ teaspoon salt

¼ teaspoon ground cinnamon

1 (6-ounce) container raspberries or 1 generous cup mixed blackberries, raspberries, and blueberries

¼ cup sliced almonds (toasted, if desired)

Honey, for drizzling

 Place the quinoa in a fine-mesh sieve and rinse under running cold water. Drain well and transfer to a medium saucepan. Add 2 cups of the almond milk, the salt, and the cinnamon. Set the pan over medium-high heat and bring to a boil, stirring occasionally. Cover the pan, reduce the heat to low, and simmer for 20 minutes without removing the lid. Turn off the heat and let stand, covered, for 5 minutes. Remove the lid and fluff the quinoa with a fork.

Divide the quinoa evenly among 4 bowls. Pour ¼ cup of the remaining almond milk over each serving, adding more if you prefer a thinner consistency. Top the quinoa with the berries and almonds, dividing them evenly among the bowls. Drizzle with honey and serve right away.

Try this!
Change up the flavors by substituting any type of fruits and nuts for the berries and almonds.

Power-Packed Fig Bars

These hearty energy bars, filled with a sweet purée of figs and dates, are great for breakfast with your favorite flavor of yogurt, and they're also a terrific snack at any time of day. You can make the dough a week ahead and store it in the refrigerator.

1¼ cups all-purpose flour, plus more for dusting

½ cup whole-wheat flour

1 teaspoon baking powder

¼ teaspoon salt

½ cup (1 stick) unsalted butter, at room temperature, plus more for greasing

¾ cup firmly packed light or dark brown sugar

1 large egg

1 teaspoon vanilla extract

8 ounces (about 1 cup) dried mission figs, stemmed and coarsely chopped

4 ounces (about ½ cup) pitted dates, chopped

¼ cup water

1 tablespoon fresh lemon juice

 In a medium bowl, whisk together the flours, baking powder, and salt. In a large bowl, using an electric mixer, beat the butter and ½ cup plus 2 tablespoons of the brown sugar on medium speed until smooth. Add the egg and vanilla and beat until combined. Scrape down the bowl. Add the flour mixture and mix on low speed until blended. Divide the dough in half and wrap each piece in plastic wrap. Refrigerate until firm, at least 1 hour or up to 1 week.

Meanwhile, put the figs and dates in a medium heatproof bowl. In a small saucepan, combine the water, remaining 2 tablespoons brown sugar, and lemon juice. Set the pan over medium heat and bring to a boil, stirring to dissolve the sugar. Pour the mixture over the fruits, cover, and let soak until cooled to room temperature, about 1 hour. Transfer the dried fruits and soaking liquid to a food processor. Purée until smooth. Transfer to a bowl, cover, and set aside.

Preheat the oven to 375°F. Butter an 8-inch square baking pan. Unwrap 1 piece of dough and place it on a lightly floured work surface. Roll out the dough to a square just larger than the pan and about ¼ inch thick, then trim with a knife into an 8-inch square. Fit the dough into the bottom of the prepared pan. Scrape the fruit purée onto the dough and spread it evenly. Roll out and trim the remaining piece of dough the same way. Lay it on top of the fruit purée.

Bake until golden brown, 20 to 25 minutes. Remove from the oven and set on a wire rack. Run a knife along the inside edge of the pan to loosen the bars. Cool completely in the pan. Turn the pan over onto a cutting board. Cut into 16 bars.

All-Star Granola

Granola is a snap to make, and the best part is that making your own allows you to customize it however you like. Love cashews or pistachios? Swap them for the almonds. Seed happy? Add a mix of pumpkin seeds and flaxseeds along with the sunflower seeds.

4 cups old-fashioned rolled oats

1 cup unsweetened coconut flakes

1 cup slivered almonds

⅓ cup shelled raw sunflower seeds

½ cup firmly packed light brown sugar

½ cup maple syrup

2 tablespoons honey

⅓ cup canola oil or coconut oil

½ teaspoon ground cinnamon

1 teaspoon salt

1 teaspoon vanilla extract

¾ cup dried blueberries, chopped dried strawberries, chopped dried cherries, or a combination

 Preheat the oven to 300°F.

In a large bowl, combine the oats, coconut, almonds, and sunflower seeds and stir well. Put the brown sugar, maple syrup, honey, oil, cinnamon, and salt in a small saucepan. Set the pan over medium-low heat and bring to a simmer, stirring until the brown sugar dissolves, about 3 minutes. Remove the pan from the heat and stir in the vanilla. Carefully pour the mixture over the oat mixture and stir until the dry ingredients are evenly moistened.

Spread the mixture into an even layer on a large rimmed cookie sheet. Bake, stirring occasionally, until the granola is golden brown, 30 to 40 minutes. Remove the cookie sheet from the oven and set it on a wire rack. Immediately sprinkle the dried fruit over the top and carefully stir it into the granola. Let cool completely, stirring every so often. The granola will keep in an airtight container at room temperature for up to 2 weeks.

Cinnamon-Spiced Oatmeal with Fruit & Nuts

Ordinary oatmeal gets a makeover with swirls of brown sugar, chewy dried fruits, and crunchy chopped nuts. Try a different topping combo every day of the week!

4 cups whole milk

2 cups old-fashioned rolled oats

1 teaspoon ground cinnamon

Big pinch of salt

4 tablespoons (½ stick) unsalted butter (optional)

2 tablespoons firmly packed light brown sugar

1 cup chopped dried fruits, such as apricots, figs, peaches, pitted dates, apples, raisins, or a combination

1 cup chopped nuts, such as almonds, pecans, walnuts, or a combination (toasted, if desired)

 In a medium saucepan, combine the milk, oats, cinnamon, and salt. Set the pan over medium-high heat and stir with a wooden spoon until the mixture begins to simmer. Reduce the heat to medium and continue to cook, stirring frequently, until the oatmeal has thickened, about 4 minutes.

Divide the oatmeal evenly among 4 bowls. Top each serving with 1 tablespoon of the butter (if using) and sprinkle with 1½ teaspoons of the brown sugar. Scatter ¼ cup of the dried fruits and ¼ cup of the nuts over each bowl and swirl with a spoon. Serve right away.

Try this!
Instead of butter and dried fruits, top the oatmeal with sliced bananas or fresh blueberries and a drizzle of cream.

Fruit Smoothies

Thanks to the combo of juicy fruits, bananas, and yogurt, these smoothies are refreshing and filling. To create layered smoothies, fill a glass half full with one flavor, then pour a second flavor over the back of a spoon to create a top layer.

BLUEBERRY-POMEGRANATE

2 ripe bananas, peeled and cut into chunks

1 cup fresh or frozen blueberries

2 tablespoons honey

1 cup cold pomegranate juice

2 cups vanilla yogurt

A few ice cubes

PINEAPPLE-PEACH

4 cups frozen peach slices

2 small ripe bananas, peeled and cut into chunks

1 cup vanilla yogurt

A few ice cubes

1 cup pineapple juice, plus more as needed

 For the blueberry-pomegranate smoothies, put the banana chunks, blueberries, and honey into a blender. Pour in the pomegranate juice and blend to a coarse purée, 30 to 45 seconds. Add the yogurt and ice and blend until smooth. Pour into glasses and serve right away.

For the pineapple-peach smoothies, put the peach slices, banana chunks, yogurt, and ice into a blender. Pour in the pineapple juice and blend until smooth, 1 to 2 minutes, adding more juice or ice as needed to create the consistency you like. Pour into glasses and serve right away.

Breakfast on the go! Keep an insulated beverage container stashed in the freezer—it will come in handy if you want to take your smoothie to go.

Eat a rainbow

Mixing different, colorful fruits not only looks super pretty, but also helps you get a variety of vitamins into one dish.

Fantastic Fruit Salad

Fruit cut into heart or star shapes makes this fruit salad so much fun. You can change out the fruits to suit your taste (see our ideas below), but make sure to include lots of different colors so that the salad looks festive and oh-so fantastic.

½ cup water

½ cup sugar

2 tablespoons fresh lime juice

2 pounds seedless watermelon, cut into ½-inch-thick slices

1 ripe mango, peeled, pitted, and cut into 1-inch chunks

½ ripe pineapple, peeled, cored, and cut into 1-inch chunks

6 cups mixed raspberries, blueberries, blackberries, and hulled and halved strawberries

½ cup fresh mint leaves, coarsely chopped, plus mint sprigs for garnish (optional)

 Combine the water and sugar in a small saucepan. Set the pan over medium heat and stir until the mixture is warm and the sugar has completely dissolved. Pour the syrup into a bowl and let cool completely. Stir in the lime juice, cover, and refrigerate until the syrup is cold, at least 2 hours or up to 1 day.

Using small (about 1½-inch diameter) star- and/or heart-shaped cookie cutters, cut out shapes from the watermelon slices, mango chunks, and pineapple chunks, making the cuts as close together as you can. Save the scraps for puréeing into smoothies (page 71).

In a large glass or ceramic bowl, combine the watermelon, mango, pineapple, and berries and gently toss to mix. Drizzle with the syrup, scatter with the chopped mint (if using), and toss very gently. Garnish with the mint sprigs, if you like, and serve right away.

Ideas for other fruits

Honeydew or cantaloupe, *seeded and cut into 1-inch chunks*

Pitted and sliced peaches, nectarines, or plums

Peeled and seeded papaya, *cut into 1-inch chunks*

Seedless green or red grapes

Pomegranate seeds

Egg-cellent
Eats

Scrambled Egg Chilaquiles

This tasty egg scramble includes a poblano chile, which can range from mild to spicy. Carefully remove its seeds before cooking so that the dish doesn't become too spicy! For a pretty finish, top each serving with minced red onion and fresh cilantro leaves.

8 large eggs

3 tablespoons whole milk

Pinch of salt

¼ cup shredded Cheddar cheese

3 corn tortillas

2 tablespoons canola oil

1 large poblano chile, seeded and cut into thin strips

2 ripe tomatoes, chopped

 In a medium bowl, whisk the eggs, milk, and salt until nice and frothy. Stir in the shredded cheese. Set aside.

Stack the tortillas and cut the stack in half, then cut each stack into wedges or crosswise into strips about ½ inch wide. Set aside.

Put the canola oil in a cast-iron skillet or large nonstick frying pan and set the pan over medium heat. Add the chile and cook, stirring often, until softened, 4 to 5 minutes. Add the tortilla wedges and cook, stirring constantly, until they begin to brown, about 2 minutes. Reduce the heat to medium-low, pour in the egg mixture, and cook, stirring often and scraping the pan bottom to prevent sticking, until the eggs are set but still moist, 2 to 3 minutes longer. Gently stir in the tomatoes and serve right away.

Breakfast Pizzas

Pizza for breakfast? Yes, please! Each individual pie is topped with an egg, making these an awesome morning meal. Add sausage, bacon, or any other toppings you like! The pizzas are best hot out of the oven, so serve each one right away.

DOUGH

1½ cups lukewarm (110°F) water

1 package (2½ teaspoons) active dry yeast

2 tablespoons extra-virgin olive oil, plus more for greasing the bowl

½ cup semolina flour

1 tablespoon salt

3 to 4 cups all-purpose flour, plus more for dusting

Cornmeal, for dusting

 To make the dough, pour the water into the bowl of a stand mixer, sprinkle in the yeast, and let stand until foamy, about 2 minutes. Add the olive oil, semolina flour, and salt. Attach the dough hook to the stand mixer and mix on medium speed until combined. Add the all-purpose flour, ½ cup at a time, and knead on medium speed until the dough is smooth but not sticky, about 10 minutes. Remove the dough from the bowl and shape it into a ball. Grease a large bowl with olive oil. Add the dough and turn to coat its entire surface with oil. Cover with a clean kitchen towel and let rise in a warm place until the dough has doubled in bulk, about 1 hour.

Use your hand to gently punch down and deflate the dough. Lightly flour a clean work surface. Turn the dough out onto the floured surface and divide it into 6 even portions. Briefly knead each portion and shape it into a ball. Leave the balls on the floured surface, spacing them about 2 inches apart. Cover with the kitchen towel and let rise until doubled in bulk, about 45 minutes.

While the dough balls rise, preheat the oven to 450°F.

Set a medium frying pan over medium-high heat and let the pan heat for about 2 minutes. Add the sausage and cook, breaking up the meat with a wooden spoon into pieces about the size of walnuts, until it's only barely pink, 7 to 8 minutes. Using a slotted spoon, transfer the sausage to a paper towel–lined plate to drain. Set the sausage aside.

Carefree crust

If you don't have time to make your owndough, you can use 32 ounces of store-bought pizza dough.

Working with 1 ball of dough at a time, use a rolling pin to roll out the dough balls to rounds about 8 inches in diameter, or use your hands to flatten and gently stretch the dough.

Dust a rimless cookie sheet with cornmeal and place a dough round on it. Top the dough with one-sixth each of the cheese, the sausage, plus any additional toppings (see box below), leaving a small circle in the center uncovered for the egg. Brush the edge of the dough with olive oil. Carefully crack 1 egg onto the center of the pizza and sprinkle the egg with a pinch each of salt and pepper. Bake until the crust is crisp and golden brown, the cheese is melted, and the egg white is set but the yolk is still soft, about 12 minutes.

Remove the pizza from the oven and, using 2 spatulas, carefully transfer it to a plate. Sprinkle with one-sixth of the green onions. Repeat with the remaining dough rounds and toppings, serving each as it's ready.

TOPPINGS

1 pound pork or chicken breakfast sausage, casings removed

8 ounces shredded mozzarella cheese

Extra-virgin olive oil, for brushing

6 large eggs

Salt and ground black pepper

3 green onions, thinly sliced

Ideas for additional toppings

Cooked crumbled bacon

Diced ham

Pepperoni slices

Cherry tomato halves

Sliced mushrooms

Thinly sliced bell peppers

Cooked diced potatoes or leftover Hash Browns (page 122)

Breakfast Burritos

Breakfast burritos are ideal for eating on the go, but they're also tons of fun at a brunch party. Set out warm tortillas and the fillings and let your guests wrap their own burritos. For a vegetarian option, replace the chorizo with cooked potatoes or black beans.

4 burrito-sized flour tortillas

8 large eggs

2 tablespoons whole milk

2 tablespoons chopped fresh cilantro

Salt and ground black pepper

Cayenne pepper (optional)

1 teaspoon canola oil

½ white onion, finely chopped

8 ounces Mexican-style (fresh) chorizo, casing removed

½ cup shredded Monterey jack cheese

Pico de Gallo (page 93) or store-bought fresh or jarred tomato salsa

1 ripe avocado, sliced

 Preheat the oven to 300°F. Stack the tortillas and wrap them in aluminum foil.

In a medium bowl, whisk the eggs, milk, cilantro, a pinch each of salt and black pepper, and a pinch of cayenne (if using) until nice and frothy, 1 to 2 minutes.

Put the canola oil in a medium nonstick frying pan and set the pan over medium heat. Add the onion, a pinch each of salt and black pepper, and a pinch of cayenne (if using). Cook, stirring occasionally, until the onion begins to soften, 3 to 4 minutes. Add the chorizo and cook, breaking it into small pieces with a wooden spoon, until the chorizo is cooked through, about 6 minutes, and the onion is soft and translucent. Reduce the heat to medium-low, pour in the eggs, and cook without stirring until the eggs just begin to set, about 1 minute. Gently stir the eggs, letting the uncooked egg run onto the surface of the pan. Continue to cook, stirring gently and constantly, until the eggs are set but still moist, 2 to 3 minutes longer. Transfer the eggs to a large plate and cover with aluminum foil.

Warm the foil-wrapped tortillas in the oven for 5 minutes. Place each tortilla on a plate and sprinkle with 2 tablespoons cheese. Spoon one-fourth of the egg mixture onto each tortilla and top with a heaping spoonful of pico de gallo and a few avocado slices. Fold the edge of the tortilla nearest you over the filling, fold in the sides, and roll away from you. Place the burritos seam side down on each plate. Serve right away.

Fill it up

You can also add cooked bacon, shredded chicken, diced potatoes, or black beans to your burritos before rolling them.

Classic Omelet

An omelet is a super-satisfying breakfast, and it's a great dinner, too. Cheddar cheese is a classic addition, but other melty cheeses—like Monterey jack, Swiss, or mozzarella—also work nicely. For extra-hearty omelets, try some of the filling ideas below.

8 large eggs

Salt and ground black pepper

4 tablespoons finely chopped fresh flat-leaf parsley, chives, cilantro, or a combination, plus more for sprinkling (optional)

2 tablespoons unsalted butter, melted

4 tablespoons shredded Cheddar cheese, plus more for sprinkling

Fillings (see box; optional)

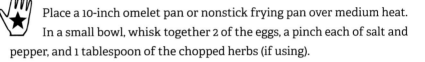 Place a 10-inch omelet pan or nonstick frying pan over medium heat. In a small bowl, whisk together 2 of the eggs, a pinch each of salt and pepper, and 1 tablespoon of the chopped herbs (if using).

Pour 1½ teaspoons of the melted butter into the pan and, using a silicone spatula, spread it evenly over the surface. Pour in the egg mixture. Using the spatula, lift the cooked eggs and gently push them toward the center, tilting the pan to allow the uncooked egg to run underneath. Repeat until the eggs cover the surface of the pan and are no longer runny, 1 to 2 minutes. Sprinkle 1 tablespoon of the cheese (and any other fillings) over the eggs and cook just until the cheese is melted and the eggs are fully set, about 1 minute longer. Using the spatula, fold the omelet in half and slide it onto a plate. Sprinkle with more cheese and herbs (if using) and serve right away. Repeat to cook 3 more omelets and serve each when it's ready.

Ideas for fillings

Sautéed fresh veggies, *such as diced tomatoes, diced zucchini, diced red onion, chopped spinach, and sliced mushrooms*

Strips of smoked salmon

Breakfast sausage or Mexican-style (fresh) chorizo, *removed from its casing and cooked*

Diced ham

Cooked crumbled bacon

Mini Frittatas with Spinach, Bacon & Cheese

A frittata is an Italian omelet that's packed with fillings. These fun two-bite frittatas are baked in a mini-muffin pan and are perfect for a brunch party, but they're also portable so you can pack them for lunch or eat them as a snack anytime and anywhere.

Unsalted butter, for greasing (optional)

1 (10-ounce) package frozen chopped spinach, thawed

4 bacon slices, thinly sliced

2 tablespoons chopped green onion

8 large eggs

2 tablespoons heavy cream

¾ cup shredded Monterey jack cheese

Pinch of salt

Pinch of ground black pepper

 Preheat the oven to 375°F. Line a 24-cup mini-muffin pan with mini foil, paper, or silicone liners, or generously grease the cups with butter.

Separate out about one-fourth of the spinach; reserve the remaining spinach for another use. Using your hands, squeeze the spinach over the sink to remove the excess water.

Set a small frying pan over medium heat. Add the bacon and cook, stirring often, until lightly browned, 3 to 4 minutes. Using a slotted spoon, transfer the bacon to a paper towel–lined plate; drain off half of the bacon fat and leave the rest in the pan. Set the pan over low heat and add the green onion. Cook, stirring occasionally, until the onion has softened, about 2 minutes. Using the slotted spoon, transfer the onion to the plate with the bacon and set aside.

In a large bowl, whisk the eggs and cream until blended. Add the cheese, spinach, and bacon–green onion mixture, season with salt and pepper, and stir to combine. Pour the egg mixture into the prepared muffin cups, dividing it evenly. Bake until the frittatas are puffy and set (when the eggs are no longer wobbly), about 10 minutes. Remove from the oven and let the frittatas cool in the pan on a wire rack for about 5 minutes, then carefully transfer them directly to the rack. Let cool for a few minutes longer and serve warm or at room temperature.

Make it zesty

Along with the spinach, you can also add 1 cup finely chopped cherry tomatoes or ½ cup finely chopped sundried tomatoes.

Cheesy Egg & Sausage Sandwiches

These breakfast sandwiches couldn't be easier to make and more irresistible to eat! For an awesome on-the-go breakfast, wrap a freshly made sandwich tightly in aluminum foil and take it with you.

6 breakfast sausage patties (thawed, if frozen)

6 slices sharp Cheddar cheese

6 English muffins, split in half

6 large eggs

⅛ teaspoon salt

Pinch of ground black pepper

2 tablespoons unsalted butter

Set a large nonstick frying pan over medium heat and let the pan heat for about 2 minutes. Add the sausage patties in a single layer, reduce the heat to medium-low, and cook until browned on the bottom, about 5 minutes. Flip the patties and cook until browned on the second sides, about 5 minutes longer. Place a slice of cheese on each patty, cover the pan, and cook until the cheese melts, about 1 minute. Transfer the patties to a paper towel–lined plate and set aside. Pour off and discard the fat in the pan and set the pan aside.

Place the English muffin halves in a toaster and toast until lightly crisped.

In a medium bowl, whisk the eggs, salt, and pepper just until nice and frothy, 1 to 2 minutes. Wipe out the frying pan with paper towels. Add the butter and set the pan over medium heat. When the butter has melted, use a silicone spatula to spread it evenly over the surface. Pour in the egg mixture and cook without stirring until it just begins to set, about 30 seconds. Using the spatula, lift the cooked edges and gently push them toward the center, tilting the pan to allow the uncooked egg to run underneath, and cook for 30 seconds. Repeat the process, then cover the pan and cook until the eggs have set into a thin omelet, about 30 seconds longer. Remove from the heat. Using the spatula, divide the omelet into 6 even wedges.

Top each of 6 muffin halves with a sausage patty, followed by a wedge of the eggs, folded to fit. Cover with remaining muffin halves and serve right away.

Egg & Cheese Breakfast Tacos

Say *buenos días* with breakfast tacos! Scrambled eggs and melted cheese are even more fun to eat when they're wrapped in warm tortillas. Store-bought fresh or jarred salsa is a fine substitute for the homemade pico de gallo.

PICO DE GALLO

2 large ripe tomatoes, seeded and chopped

½ cup finely chopped yellow onion

3 tablespoons minced fresh cilantro

1 tablespoon fresh lime juice

Salt

TACOS

8 (6-inch) corn or flour tortillas

8 large eggs

Salt and ground black pepper

2 tablespoons extra-virgin olive oil

1 small yellow onion, chopped

1 cup shredded Monterey jack or Cheddar cheese

 To make the pico de gallo, in a medium bowl, combine the tomatoes, onion, cilantro, and lime juice. Season to taste with salt. Cover and let stand at room temperature for at least 30 minutes or up to 3 hours.

Preheat the oven to 300°F. To make the tacos, stack the tortillas and wrap them in aluminum foil. In a medium bowl, whisk the eggs, ¾ teaspoon salt, and ¼ teaspoon pepper until just nice and frothy, 1 to 2 minutes.

Put the olive oil in a large nonstick frying pan and set the pan over medium-high heat. When the olive oil is shimmering, add the onion and cook, stirring often, until the onion has softened, about 2 minutes. Sprinkle with salt and pepper and reduce the heat to medium-low. Pour in the eggs and cook without stirring until they just begin to set, about 20 seconds. Using a silicone spatula, scrape along the bottom and sides of the pan and fold the egg mixture toward the center. Continue to cook, scraping and folding the mixture, until the eggs form very moist curds, about 3 minutes longer. Transfer to a large plate and cover with aluminum foil to keep warm. Meanwhile, place the foil-wrapped tortillas in the oven to warm for 5 minutes.

Remove the tortillas from the oven and unwrap them. Place the tortillas on plates. Spoon the egg mixture onto the tortillas, dividing it evenly. Sprinkle with cheese, top with pico de gallo, and serve right away.

Toad in a Hole

Eggs with toast are a great breakfast, but eggs *in* toast are even better!
To cut out the hole from the bread slices, you can use a plain round cookie
cutter or get creative with playful shapes like stars, hearts, or flowers.

**4 slices sandwich
bread**

**2 tablespoons
unsalted butter,
at room temperature,
plus more for cooking**

4 large eggs

**Salt and ground
black pepper**

 Spread both sides of each bread slice with butter, dividing the butter evenly. Using a 3-inch round cutter, cut a circle out of the center of each slice of bread; reserve the cutout.

Set a 12-inch nonstick frying pan or griddle over medium heat and let the pan heat for about 2 minutes. Add about 2 teaspoons butter and, using a silicone spatula, spread it evenly over the surface. Place the bread, including the cutout circles, in a single layer in the pan; work in batches if you can't fit all of the bread in the pan at one time. Cook for 1 minute, then slide a thin spatula under each slice of bread and turn them over. Turn the cutout circles, too. Crack an egg into the hole in each slice of bread and sprinkle it lightly with salt and pepper. Cook until the egg whites are opaque and the yolks are just set but still runny, about 2 to 3 minutes, or longer if desired.

Using the spatula, slide each "toad in a hole" carefully onto a serving plate and place a cutout alongside it. Serve right away.

Crowd-
Pleasers

Breakfast Quesadillas

Filled with scrambled eggs, roasted red bell peppers, and green onions, this breakfast version of a mealtime favorite is an awesome and power-packed way to start your day.

1 ripe avocado

4 large eggs

Pinch of salt

Pinch of ground black pepper

1 tablespoon olive oil

½ cup chopped jarred roasted red bell peppers, drained well

2 tablespoons thinly sliced green onion

2 (10-inch) flour tortillas

⅔ cup shredded sharp Cheddar cheese

Sour cream, for serving

Pico de Gallo (page 93) or store-bought fresh or jarred salsa, for serving

 Preheat the oven to 200°F. Cut the avocado in half lengthwise. Using a spoon, scoop out the pit and discard it. Carefully peel off the skin and cut each half lengthwise into thin slices. Cover the slices with plastic wrap to prevent them from browning.

In a small bowl, whisk the eggs, salt, and pepper until frothy, 1 to 2 minutes. Put the oil in a medium nonstick frying pan and set the pan over medium heat. Add the eggs to the pan and cook without stirring until they just begin to set, about 20 seconds. Using a silicone spatula, scrape along the bottom and sides of the pan and fold the eggs toward the center. Add the peppers and green onion and continue to cook, scraping and folding the eggs, until the eggs form moist curds, about 1 minute. Remove the pan from the heat and set aside.

Set another medium frying pan over medium heat. Have a cookie sheet ready. Place 1 tortilla in the pan and heat until warmed, about 1 minute. Flip the tortilla and sprinkle the bottom half with ⅓ cup of the cheese. Top the cheese evenly with half of the egg mixture. Fold the tortilla in half in the frying pan to cover the filling. Continue cooking until the underside begins to brown, about 1 minute. Carefully flip and cook the second side until it begins to brown, about 1 minute longer. Transfer to the cookie sheet and keep warm in the oven. Repeat with the remaining ingredients to make another quesadilla.

Cut each quesadilla into 3 or 4 wedges and divide among individual plates. Top with avocado slices, a dollop of sour cream, and pico de gallo. Serve right away.

Breakfast Biscuit Sandwiches

Biscuit sandwiches are hearty and filling yet dainty enough for a tea party–inspired brunch. Create a biscuit bar by setting out the little breads and fillings (try any of our favorite ideas below) and letting guests make their own sandwiches.

2 cups all-purpose flour, plus more for dusting

2½ teaspoons baking powder

½ teaspoon salt

6 tablespoons (¾ stick) cold unsalted butter, cut into ½-inch cubes

¾ cup whole milk

Fillings of your choice (see box)

 Preheat the oven to 425°F. Line a large cookie sheet with parchment paper.

In a large bowl, whisk together the flour, baking powder, and salt. Scatter the butter cubes over the flour mixture and toss to coat. Using a pastry cutter or 2 dinner knives, cut the butter into the dry ingredients until the mixture forms crumbs the size of small peas. Pour in the milk and stir with a fork or rubber spatula just until the mixture is evenly moistened and a loose dough forms.

Lightly dust a clean work surface with flour and turn the dough out onto it. Using your hands, gently press the dough until it holds together. Using a light touch or a lightly floured rolling pin, press or roll the dough into a rough rectangle about ¾ inch thick. Using a chef's knife, cut the dough into 8 square biscuits, cutting straight down and lifting straight up with each cut. Place the biscuits on the prepared cookie sheet, spacing them 1 inch apart.

Bake until golden brown, 15 to 18 minutes. Remove from the oven and let cool on a wire rack for about 10 minutes. Split horizontally, fill, and serve right away.

Ideas for fillings

Easy Fried Eggs *(page 27)*

Sliced Cheddar or Swiss cheese

Maple-Glazed Bacon *(page 120)*

Chopped green onions

Sliced avocados or tomatoes

Butter and jam or honey

PB&J Panini

Take PB&J to a whole new level by spreading peanut butter and jam on slices of buttered cinnamon bread and toasting the sandwich in a panini press (or on a nonstick frying pan or grill pan) until the outside is crisp and the filling is warm and oozy.

4 (½-inch-thick) slices cinnamon or cinnamon-raisin bread

1 tablespoon unsalted butter, at room temperature

¼ cup smooth or chunky natural peanut butter

2 tablespoons fruit jam (use your favorite type)

 Spread 1 side of each bread slice with butter, evenly dividing the butter. Spread each unbuttered side of bread with 1 tablespoon of the peanut butter. On 2 of the bread slices, spread 1 tablespoon of the jam on the peanut butter. Place the remaining 2 bread slices on top, peanut butter sides down, and press gently.

If using a panini press, preheat it. Place the sandwiches in the press, close the top plate, and cook until the bread is golden brown and toasted and the filling is warmed, 2 to 4 minutes.

If cooking on the stovetop, set a medium grill pan or nonstick frying pan over medium heat and let it heat for 3 minutes. Place the sandwiches in the pan and cook, turning once, until golden brown on both sides, 2 to 3 minutes per side. As the sandwiches cook, use a wide metal spatula to press them down once or twice on each side.

Transfer the panini to a cutting board and cut each one in half diagonally. Serve right away.

Bread-and-Butter Pudding with Pears

In this rich and creamy breakfast treat, layers of buttery bread soaked in custard are baked on top of sweet sautéed pears. You can easily swap out the pears for apples. Or leave out the ground cinnamon and substitute cinnamon-raisin bread for the challah.

5 tablespoons unsalted butter, at room temperature, plus more for greasing the baking dish

4 ripe but firm pears, such as Anjou or Comice, peeled, cored, and cut into eighths

⅓ cup plus 2 teaspoons granulated sugar

6 (½-inch-thick) slices day-old challah bread

2 cups whole milk

4 large eggs

1 teaspoon vanilla extract

½ teaspoon ground cinnamon

Pinch of salt

1 tablespoon powdered sugar

 Generously butter a 2-quart shallow glass or ceramic baking dish.

Put 2 tablespoons of the butter in a large frying pan and set the pan over medium-high heat. When the butter has melted, add the pears and cook, stirring occasionally, until they begin to brown, about 5 minutes. Sprinkle with the 2 teaspoons granulated sugar and continue to cook, stirring occasionally, until the pears begin to caramelize, about 3 minutes longer. Transfer the pears to the prepared baking dish and spread them in an even layer.

Preheat the oven to 325°F. Spread 1 side of each of the bread slices with the remaining 3 tablespoons butter, dividing the butter evenly. Cut each bread slice in half. Arrange the bread over the pears, buttered side down, in overlapping rows. In a large bowl, whisk together the milk, eggs, vanilla, cinnamon, salt, and the remaining ⅓ cup granulated sugar. Pour the mixture over the bread. Gently press down on the bread with a spatula to submerge it in the egg mixture. Let stand at room temperature until the bread has soaked up the egg mixture, 10 to 15 minutes.

Bake until a knife inserted into the center of the bread pudding comes out clean, 30 to 35 minutes. Remove from the oven and let cool on a wire rack for 5 minutes. Put the powdered sugar in a fine-mesh sieve and lightly dust it over the top. Serve warm.

Croque Monsieur

A croque monsieur is the French version of a grilled ham-and-cheese sandwich. Serve these with a fork and knife because a rich, super-yummy cheese sauce is poured over the grilled sandwiches just before they're topped with more cheese and broiled. Ooh la la!

SANDWICHES

2 tablespoons unsalted butter, at room temperature

8 slices sandwich bread or brioche

8 thin slices ham

SAUCE

2 tablespoons unsalted butter

2 tablespoons all-purpose flour

1½ teaspoons salt

⅛ teaspoon cayenne pepper

1½ cups whole milk

¾ cup shredded Gruyère cheese

To make the sandwiches, spread 1 side of each bread slice with butter, evenly dividing the butter. Turn 4 bread slices buttered side down, arrange 2 slices of ham on each, and top with the remaining 4 bread slices, buttered side up. Set the sandwiches aside.

To make the sauce, put the butter in a medium saucepan and set the pan over medium heat. When the butter has melted, remove the pan from the heat. Add the flour, salt, and cayenne pepper and whisk until well blended. Return the pan to medium heat and slowly whisk in the milk. Bring the mixture to a simmer, whisking constantly, then reduce the heat to low and cook, whisking frequently, until the sauce is smooth and thick, about 15 minutes. Add ¼ cup of the cheese, whisk to combine, and remove the pan from the heat.

Position an oven rack about 6 inches from the upper heat source and preheat the broiler. Line a rimmed cookie sheet with aluminum foil.

Set a large nonstick frying pan over medium heat and let it heat for 3 minutes. Place the sandwiches in the pan and cook, turning once, until golden brown on both sides, about 4 minutes per side. Transfer the sandwiches to the prepared cookie sheet and pour about ¼ cup of the cheese sauce over each sandwich. Top the sandwiches with the remaining ½ cup cheese, dividing it evenly. Broil the sandwiches until the sauce bubbles and the cheese is golden, 4 to 5 minutes. Remove from the broiler, transfer to plates, and serve right away.

Peach-Blackberry Crisp with Yogurt

Here's a secret: if you serve yogurt instead of ice cream with a fruity dessert, you can call it breakfast! This fruit crisp can be made in a big baking dish and served family style. Or, for a fancier option, you can make individual servings in ramekins (small ceramic cups).

4 ripe but firm peaches, peeled and sliced

1 cup blackberries

½ cup old-fashioned rolled oats

½ cup firmly packed light brown sugar

¼ cup all-purpose flour

¼ cup finely chopped almonds or pecans

½ teaspoon ground cinnamon

¼ teaspoon ground nutmeg

¼ teaspoon salt

6 tablespoons (¾ stick) unsalted butter, at room temperature, cut into ½-inch pieces

1 cup plain or vanilla yogurt, for serving

 Preheat the oven to 375°F.

In a medium bowl, toss the peaches and blackberries gently to combine. Transfer the fruit mixture to a 9-by-13-inch glass or ceramic baking dish and spread it in an even layer or divide it evenly among eight 1-cup ramekins.

In another medium bowl, stir together the oats, brown sugar, flour, nuts, cinnamon, nutmeg, and salt. Add the butter and, using your fingertips, rub the butter into the oat mixture until well blended and clumpy. Scatter the topping evenly over the fruit. If you're using ramekins, set them on a rimmed cookie sheet.

Bake until the juices are bubbling and the topping is richly browned, 30 to 35 minutes. Remove from the oven and let cool on a wire rack until warm, about 15 minutes. Serve the ramekins with a dollop of yogurt on top of each one, or scoop servings from the baking dish onto plates and top each with a spoonful of yogurt.

Tomato & Mozzarella Strata

The word *strata* means "layers," and this easy, all-in-one breakfast dish is a savory bread pudding that has layers of bread, cheese, and tomatoes. You can swap the country-style bread for a baguette, challah, or even English muffins.

Unsalted butter, for greasing the baking dish

6 large eggs

2 cups whole milk

1 cup heavy cream

2 tablespoons grated Parmesan cheese

Salt and ground black pepper

1 loaf country-style bread, cut into ½-inch-thick slices

2 cups shredded whole-milk mozzarella cheese

3 medium tomatoes, diced

 Butter a 13-by-9-inch glass or ceramic baking dish. In a medium bowl, whisk together the eggs, milk, cream, Parmesan, and a pinch each of salt and pepper.

Arrange half of the bread slices in a single layer in the bottom of the prepared baking dish. Pour half of the egg mixture over the bread and top with half each of the mozzarella and tomatoes. Repeat the layering with the remaining ingredients. Let the strata stand at room temperature for 30 minutes, occasionally pressing it down with a spatula to keep the bread submerged. Preheat the oven to 350°F.

Bake for 30 minutes. Remove the strata from the oven and, using the spatula, press down on the top layer of bread. Continue to bake until the strata is golden brown and puffed, about 30 minutes longer. Remove from the oven and let cool on a wire rack for about 10 minutes. Cut into squares and serve warm.

Ideas for add-ins

Fresh herbs, *such as thyme, flat-leaf parsley, or sage, chopped and added to the egg mixture*

Italian sausage or breakfast sausage, *removed from its casing, cooked, and scattered over the bottom bread layer*

Slices of ham, *placed on top of the bottom bread layer*

Crack carefully
To avoid eggshells in the dish, crack the eggs into an extra ramekin, then slide them into the prepared ramekins.

Individual Baked Eggs with Spinach & Ham

Individual baked eggs might seem fancy, but they're so simple to prepare and are perfect for a weekend brunch party since this recipe is easy to double. Serve these eggs with strips of toast or English muffins for dipping into the ooey-gooey centers.

1 tablespoon unsalted butter, plus more for greasing the ramekins

1½ pounds baby spinach, rinsed but not dried

1 teaspoon extra-virgin olive oil

3 ounces ham, chopped

¾ cup plus 4 teaspoons heavy cream

Salt and ground black pepper

4 large eggs

4 teaspoons grated Parmesan cheese

 Preheat the oven to 350°F. Butter four ¾-cup ramekins.

Put the 1 tablespoon butter in a large saucepan and set the pan over medium heat. When the butter has melted, add the spinach one handful add a time, stirring until the leaves are wilted before adding another handful. Cook until all of the spinach is tender, about 3 minutes. Pour the spinach into a colander and press on it with a wooden spoon to remove excess liquid. Transfer to a cutting board and coarsely chop.

Put the olive oil in the same saucepan and set the pan over medium heat. Add the ham and cook, stirring occasionally, until heated through, about 2 minutes. Add the spinach and the ¾ cup cream and bring to a boil. Cook, stirring often, until the cream has thickened and reduced to a few tablespoons, about 4 minutes. Season to taste with salt and pepper. Divide the mixture evenly among the prepared ramekins. Break an egg into each ramekin. Sprinkle each with a little salt and pepper and drizzle with 1 teaspoon of the remaining cream. Carefully arrange the ramekins on a rimmed cookie sheet.

Bake until the egg whites are opaque and the yolks have firm edges but are still soft in the center, about 15 minutes; watch carefully to avoid overcooking. Remove from the oven and sprinkle each serving with 1 teaspoon of the Parmesan. Serve right away.

Tasty
Extras

Flavored Cream Cheese Six Ways

Making your own flavored cream cheese couldn't be easier. With just a few simple ingredients, you can whip up a tasty spread to spruce up your morning bagel or amp up after-school snacks for your friends.

1 (8-ounce) container spreadable cream cheese

Flavor mix-ins (see box)

Put the cream cheese and the flavor mix-ins (excluding those that must be stirred in by hand) in a small food processor and pulse until well combined. Transfer to an airtight container, add any mix-ins that must be stirred in by hand, and mix with a rubber spatula or spoon. Cover and refrigerate until ready to use.

Ideas for flavor mix-ins

Pineapple: *½ cup finely chopped peeled and cored pineapple and 1 teaspoon agave or honey*

Strawberry: *⅓ cup hulled and finely chopped strawberries and 1 tablespoon strawberry jam*

Orange-Pomegranate: *finely grated zest of 1 orange and 1 teaspoon agave or honey; by hand, stir in ¼ cup fresh pomegranate seeds*

Cinnamon-Raisin: *¼ teaspoon ground cinnamon and 2 teaspoons agave or honey; by hand, stir in 3 tablespoons raisins or currants*

Chive: *2 tablespoons chopped fresh chives*

Sun-Dried Tomato–Basil: *2 tablespoons chopped oil-packed sun-dried tomatoes and ¼ cup loosely packed chopped fresh basil leaves*

Strawberry Refrigerator Jam

Traditional homemade jam requires a canning process so it can be stored in jars at room temperature. But this recipe is for easy-to-make strawberry jam that is stored in the refrigerator. It will keep for up to 2 weeks, but it'll be eaten up long before then!

1 pound strawberries

1 cup sugar

2 tablespoons fresh lemon juice

 Put the berries on a cutting board. Using a paring knife, cut out the stem and core from the center of each berry. Slice the berries and put them in a medium saucepan.

Place a small plate in the freezer to chill. Fill a medium bowl about halfway with ice water and place a small stainless-steel bowl in the ice water.

Add the sugar and lemon juice to the berries and set the pan over medium heat. Cook, stirring constantly, until the sugar dissolves, and then reduce the heat to medium-low. Continue to cook, stirring occasionally, until the berries have softened and the juices have thickened, about 10 minutes. To check if the jam is ready, remove the chilled saucer from the freezer. Spoon about 1 teaspoon of the strawberry liquid onto the saucer and let stand for 15 seconds. If the liquid thickens to a jam-like consistency, the jam is ready. If not, continue to cook for 1 to 2 minutes longer.

Pour the jam into the stainless-steel bowl set in the bowl of ice water and let stand until cooled and thickened. Serve at room temperature or chilled.

Honeyed Whole-Wheat Bread

Homemade bread beats the flavor and texture of the store-bought kind. This slightly sweet and buttery loaf is great for breakfast toast and all of your favorite sandwiches.

2¾ cups all-purpose flour

4¾ cups whole-wheat flour

2½ cups lukewarm (110˚F) whole milk

2 tablespoons (about 3 packets) active dry yeast

½ cup honey

1½ teaspoons salt

½ cup (1 stick) unsalted butter, at room temperature, cut into ½-inch pieces, plus more for greasing the pans

In a medium bowl, stir together the flours and reserve 1 cup. Pour the milk into the bowl of a stand mixer, sprinkle in the yeast, and let stand until foamy, about 2 minutes. Whisk until the yeast dissolves, add the honey and salt, and let stand for 5 minutes. Whisk again to combine. Add the flour mixture and stir to combine; the mixture will be dry and flaky. Add the butter and, using the dough hook, knead on medium speed until the dough is smooth and elastic, about 10 minutes, adding only as much reserved flour as needed to prevent sticking. Transfer the dough to a clean work surface and knead briefly. Shape it into a ball and return it to the mixer. Cover with plastic wrap and let rise in a warm place until doubled in bulk, 2 to 2½ hours.

Preheat the oven to 375˚F. Butter two 8-by-4-inch loaf pans. Gently punch down and deflate the dough. Turn the dough out onto a clean work surface, cut in half, flatten each into a rectangle about 2 inches thick and 8 inches long, then roll each rectangle lengthwise into a log shape, pressing firmly as you go. Pinch each seam to seal and place 1 log, seam side down, in each pan. Cover the pans loosely with plastic wrap and let rise in a warm place until the dough is 1 inch above the rim of the pan, about 45 minutes.

Bake until the loaves are golden brown and sound hollow when tapped with a finger, 35 to 40 minutes. Remove from the oven and let cool in the pans on a wire rack for about 5 minutes. Turn the loaves out onto the rack, turn them upright, and let cool completely. Cut into slices for serving.

Maple-Glazed Bacon

If you like to drizzle a little extra maple syrup to the side of your pancakes for dipping your bacon, you know how good the flavors of maple and bacon taste together. The combination of sweet, salty, and crunchy is a knockout!

12 slices thick-cut bacon

2 tablespoons pure maple syrup

½ teaspoon ground black pepper (optional)

 Preheat the oven to 400°F.

Place a cooling rack inside a large rimmed baking sheet. Lay the bacon slices in a single layer on the cooling rack. Bake until the bacon is barely crisp and lightly browned, 15 to 20 minutes. Carefully drain off and discard the fat from the cookie sheet.

Brush the bacon slices with 1 tablespoon of the maple syrup and sprinkle with half of the pepper (if using). Return to the oven and bake until glazed and shiny, about 2½ minutes. Remove from the oven and, using tongs, flip over the bacon slices. Brush the second sides with the remaining 1 tablespoon syrup and sprinkle with the remaining pepper. Bake again until glazed and shiny, about 2 minutes longer. Remove from the oven and transfer the bacon to a serving platter. Let cool for 2 to 3 minutes to allow the bacon to crisp up. Serve warm.

Upgraded

This irresistible, sticky bacon is made crispier and healthier by cooking it on a rack, so that the fat drips off.

Hash Browns

Nothing goes better with eggs and bacon than hash browns. Potatoes contain a lot of moisture, so in order for them to brown and crisp nicely, the shredded spuds must be wrapped in a kitchen towel and squeezed before frying.

1 tablespoon unsalted butter

1 yellow onion, chopped

1 green or red bell pepper, seeded and chopped

Pinch of salt

Pinch of ground black pepper

1½ pounds russet potatoes, peeled

4 tablespoons canola oil

 Put the butter in a heavy-bottomed frying pan and place over medium heat. When the butter has melted, add the onion and bell pepper and cook, stirring occasionally, until the vegetables are tender, about 10 minutes. Season with salt and pepper. Transfer to a bowl and set the pan aside.

Shred the potatoes on the large holes of a box grater. Line a colander with a clean kitchen towel and set the colander in the sink. Transfer the potatoes to the prepared colander, gather the edges of the kitchen towel, and twist tightly to squeeze out the moisture. Set the towel with the potatoes in the colander and let drain for 15 minutes. Squeeze again, then transfer the potatoes to a large bowl. Add 1½ teaspoons salt and ¼ teaspoon pepper and mix well.

Put 2 tablespoons of the canola oil in the same pan and set over medium-high heat. Add the potatoes in an even layer. Reduce the heat to medium, cover, and cook until the potatoes are golden brown and crisp on the bottom, about 6 minutes. Using a wide spatula, slide the potato cake onto a plate. Place an upside-down plate on top. Hold the plates together and flip them over. Lift off the top plate; the browned side of the potatoes now faces up. Put the remaining 2 tablespoons canola oil in the pan. Slide the potatoes back into the pan and cook over medium heat until golden brown and crisp on the second side, about 6 minutes. Slide the potatoes onto a platter. Return the onion mixture to the pan and cook over medium heat, stirring often, until heated through, about 1 minute. Heap the onion mixture onto the potatoes and serve right away.

Fresh Mint Tisane

A tisane is an aromatic herbal or flower tea that's usually sipped for its health benefits. This tisane is energizing and invigorating, so it's the perfect hot beverage for mornings when you need fresh, minty flavors to jump-start the day.

2 bunches fresh mint, washed and dried

Sugar, for serving (optional)

Put the mint in a teapot. In a teakettle or small saucepan, bring 6 cups of water to a boil over high heat. Pour the water into the teapot and let steep for 3 minutes for a mild-flavored tisane or for up to 5 minutes for a stronger mint flavor.

Pour the tisane through a tea strainer or fine-mesh sieve into cups or mugs. Serve right away, passing sugar at the table, if you like.

Try this!
Add 2 bunches fresh lemon verbena to the teapot with the mint.

Whipped Hot Chocolate

Bet you didn't think it was possible to make hot chocolate even better than it already is. This version includes a bit of cinnamon and actual chocolate—not just cocoa powder—for terrific flavor, and it's whisked like crazy for frothy, amazing mugfuls.

2 cups low-fat or whole milk

4 teaspoons unsweetened Dutch-process cocoa powder, plus more for sprinkling

4 teaspoons sugar

8 ounces bittersweet chocolate, finely chopped

¼ teaspoon salt

¼ teaspoon ground cinnamon

Whipped cream, for serving (optional)

 In a small saucepan, combine the milk, cocoa powder, and sugar. Set the pan over medium heat and whisk vigorously until the sugar dissolves and the mixture is warmed through. Add the chocolate, salt, and cinnamon and continue to whisk vigorously until the mixture is frothy, smooth, and hot, about 4 minutes.

Pour the hot chocolate into cups or mugs. Top each cup with whipped cream (if using), sprinkle with cocoa powder, and serve right away.

Try this!
Scoop vanilla ice cream into the hot chocolate before topping with whipped cream.

Chai

Did you know that chai, the milky spiced tea of Indian origin, is easy to make at home? And it will fill your kitchen with a wonderful aroma. You can make the chai a day or two ahead, refrigerate it, and then reheat it in a saucepan over medium heat.

2 (1½-inch) cinnamon sticks

8 green cardamom pods

8 black cardamom pods

20 whole cloves

4 black peppercorns

10 thin slices peeled fresh ginger

3 cups water

1⅓ cups whole milk

¼ cup sugar

2 tablespoons plus 2 teaspoons decaffeinated Darjeeling or other decaffeinated black tea leaves

In a saucepan, combine the cinnamon sticks, green and black cardamom pods, cloves, peppercorns, and ginger slices. Pour in the water, set the pan over medium heat, and bring to a boil. Cover, reduce the heat to low, and simmer until the liquid is aromatic, about 10 minutes. Add the milk and sugar and bring back to a simmer over medium heat. Add the tea leaves and stir to combine. Remove from the heat, cover, and let stand for 3 minutes for a mild tea flavor or for up to 5 minutes for a stronger chai.

Pour the chai through a tea strainer or fine-mesh sieve into cups or mugs and serve right away.

Coffee-Free Latte

Rooibos tea, also known as "red tea," is an herbal caffeine-free beverage with a bold, toasty taste. We like to steep it until it has a really robust flavor, sweeten it with a little honey and some frothy warm milk, and sprinkle a dash of cinnamon over the top.

2 cups water

4 rooibos tea bags

½ cinnamon stick (optional)

½ cup whole milk

Honey or agave syrup

Ground cinnamon, for sprinkling

 Pour the water into a small saucepan and set the pan over medium-high heat. Bring the water to a boil and add the tea bags and cinnamon stick (if using). For a mild tea flavor, remove the pan from the heat, cover, and let steep for 3 minutes. For a stronger tea flavor, reduce the heat to low, cover, and simmer for 5 minutes.

While the tea steeps, pour the milk into another small saucepan. Set the pan over medium-low heat and warm the milk until steaming. Remove the pan from the heat. Using a small whisk, rapidly whisk the milk until it's frothy.

Remove and discard the tea bags and cinnamon stick from the tea and pour the tea into 2 large mugs, dividing it evenly. Add honey to taste and stir to combine. Evenly divide the frothy milk between the mugs. Sprinkle the tops with ground cinnamon and serve right away.

Index

weldon**owen**

1045 Sansome Street, Suite 100, San Francisco, CA 94111
www.weldonowen.com

Weldon Owen is a division of Bonnier Publishing USA

WELDON OWEN, INC.

President & Publisher Roger Shaw
VP, Sales & Marketing Amy Kaneko
Finance Manager Philip Paulick
Associate Publisher Amy Marr
Associate Editor Emma Rudolph
Project Editor Alexis Mersel

Creative Director Kelly Booth
Associate Art Director Lisa Berman
Senior Production Designer Rachel Lopez Metzger
Production Director Chris Hemesath
Associate Production Director Michelle Duggan
Imaging Manager Don Hill

Photographer Nicole Hill Gerulat
Food Stylists Tara Bench, Erin Quon
Prop Stylists Veronica Olson, Ethel Brennan
Hair & Makeup Kathy Hill

AMERICAN GIRL *BREAKFAST & BRUNCH*

Conceived and produced by Weldon Owen, Inc.
In collaboration with Williams Sonoma, Inc.
3250 Van Ness Avenue, San Francisco, CA 94109

A WELDON OWEN PRODUCTION

Printed and bound in China

First printed in 2017
10 9 8 7 6 5 4 3 2

Library of Congress Cataloging
in Publication data is available

ISBN 13: 978-1-68188-244-4

ACKNOWLEDGMENTS

Weldon Owen wishes to thank the following people for their generous support to help produce this book:
Matt Araquistain, Mary Bench, Lesley Bruynesteyn, Gloria Geller, Lindsey Hargett,
Alexa Hyman, Kim Laidlaw, Rachel Markowitz, A'Lissa Olson, Taylor Olson, Elizabeth Parson,
Jennifer Paul, Gracie Smith, Kristen Tate, Nathalie van Empel, and Dawn Yanagihara

A VERY SPECIAL THANK YOU TO:

Our models: Vanessa Bryant, Mimi Craven, Nyomi Houston, Ashleigh Larsen, Ava Larsen, Bronson Larsen,
David Larsen, Amarech Mendez, Lily Miller, Abigail Mindes, Adeline Phinney, Zaiden Rosenthal, Alexa Vasquez

Our locations: Sandra Lee & Sara Ward
Our prop resources: Rice by Rice
Our clothing resources: Tuchinda Design (tuchindadesign.com) and Sant and Abel (santandabel.com)